Positive Thoughts Will Change Your Life

Tony Palermo

ISBN-13: 978-1544734132

ISBN-10: 1544734131

Cover design by Dennis Wickes

DEDICATION

This book is dedicated to anyone who wishes to change his or her life.

CONTENTS

ACKNOWLEDGMENTS

Thank you Gary Quinn for writing the foreword to this book. You are a great person and so giving of your time and energy.

Dennis Wickes, thank you for a great cover design, I totally love it. You did an amazing job.

I would also like to thank Lisa Kitter, and Nancy Rarick for taking the time to review this book.

Foreword

I first met Tony several years ago. As I do with most clients, I worked with Tony one-on-one. I served as his life coach and mentor. While working with Tony, I saw his true thirst and desire to be of service and actually help others. While committed to his own work with his own life coaching, he made a unique choice to begin his journey to actually become a life coach himself. His passion to help others is inspiring.

The phrase that comes to mind is "you can't give what you don't have." In a quest to become the best life coach possible, Tony dove head first into one-on-one life coaching sessions with me. It is with this same energy and spirit that he is able to give generously and without hesitation to his clients. While his eye was on the prize, Tony obtained his life coaching credential from the Touchstone for Life Coaching Program. I know that the dedication and commitment with which Tony applied himself to his own healing has made him a phenomenal life coach.

This book reflects the journey that every soul must take to authentically be of service to others. The author came out of his own life coaching work with such drive and focus that he became a life coach with ease and fluidity.

This book contains tools to help you take command of your life which starts with your thinking. If you are looking for a champion who understands the challenges and the rewards of self-transformation, you have found one in Tony. He believes in the power of self-transformation and knows first-hand that it is possible for you.

This book is a guide that offers support and patience through one's self-transformation process. It is a wonderful resource because of the passion and true love with which the author wrote it. This passion comes from his own experience and ups and downs. This makes him not only a great resource but also a very valid one.

The commitment needed through one's personal healing process and the commitment to becoming a formal ambassador through another's healing process are similar. As a graduate of Touchstone for Life Coaching Program, the author has demonstrated his commitment and tenacity. The person who has healed himself and then wants to help others achieve the same healing is a unique and generous soul.

The generosity and the sincerity of the author can be felt on every page of this book. This book is timely as humanity moves into a stage of greater compassion and empathy.

The specific section that clarifies negative and positive affirmations is what I find most helpful. In this section the author makes it very clear that one can be affirming the negative and not even be aware of their behavior. There is nothing more potent than an author, healer or teacher who helps us recognize the things that we take for granted. This section will help one take greater responsibility for such behaviors that demand more attentiveness if self-transformation is to take place.

The tools included in *Positive Thoughts Will Change Your Life* are effective and efficient. In this great age of technology, efficiency can be demanded even in the healing process. I am very excited for you to access the tools within Tony Palermo's new book. Tony now shares his teachings with clients worldwide. He also writes a monthly blog for The Huffington Post and Thrive Global full of practical steps and actions for living your best life. He is a force for good and proactive change on our planet. Both his book and blog demonstrate this truth.

Gary Quinn, Los Angeles

Gary Quinn is a bestselling author of *The Yes Frequency: Master a Positive Belief System and Achieve Mindfulness*, and the founder of the Touchstone For Life Coaching Certification Program ® which trains, transforms and empowers individuals to create fulfilling lives. People from all walks of life including entertainers, athletes, and corporate leaders have embraced his teachings. Among his many clients are Academy Award and Grammy winners, and Olympic Gold medalists. Among his corporate clients are MSNBC, Mattel Toys, Diesel and Indigo.

Introduction

Change is the one unchanging and forever-enduring aspect of life. Change is and will always be ever-present and withstanding. It is both the acceptance and full embracing of this truth that shapes and defines us. The high and low tides of existence are all predicated on change and the management of change.

At times, change demands that we give more than we believe that we have, or more than we want to give. No matter where one is in life, the challenge of change remains. Some are better equipped mentally, emotionally, and/or physically to handle situations that beckon change forth. All have the ability to become better equipped to manage change.

Changing non-optimal habits, behaviors, attitudes, feelings, thoughts, etc., into productive and beneficial ones, can feel far-fetched and overwhelming. This book offers support, tools, and insights into how to create and sustain these very types of change.

Change might not always be pleasant but it will always be worth it.

Heart-lasting, enduring, and meaningful change takes time. Real life is not always neat and tidy. Sometimes it is plain messy— quite often it is very messy. But, it does not mean we stop living.

The true magic lies in embracing and committing with discipline to the *creation of change*.

The *creation of change*—however that specifically speaks to you—will always be a worthy treasure to unearth. Unearthing and forming new thinking and new behaviors might not be an easy task, but I can tell you, it will always be worth it.

The purpose of this book is to help you learn to create new thinking that will then lead to new behaviors. With commitment and application of the step-by-step advice, you will learn how to affirm positive things for your life. You will then be able to grow into a space of true consistency from this foundation.

This is my intention for you and for all the clients that I work with in my life coaching business.

We are all students of life. Literally we are students. This may be a cliché, but it is truth. Students have a curriculum. Students take time to study and learn. Students take tests. And students have tutors, study guides, and notes to help!

This book is simply a study guide to aid you with creating the life you want.

Here in this book are items to help you live a more positive and productive life. I may not have uncovered all the secrets of the universe, but that's not a requirement for living a happy life.

I want you to commit yourself to the continual improvement of your life. Commit to being a *student* of life, willing and able to learn, to grow, refine experiences, and to CHANGE.

No matter what, never EVER give up on working to change your life for the better.

The intention has been set here to aid you in the creation of the life you truly want. With commitment and focus, this can be done. Believe, Commit, and Achieve Your Change.

Chapter 1 – Choice

The inherent faculty of free will is the most defining aspect of life. The power of choice shapes every part of our existence. In this era of technological overload, it is easy to forget that we remain the ones in control of our own lives. With so many distractions—be it social media or our very own fears and doubts—the power of choice will always be superior to all things.

We are higher beings with the ability of discernment. We have the capacity to make decisions consciously or unconsciously. This ability is often underrated and undervalued. We often lack the foresight of the short-term and long-term effects of our decisions. This leads us to take for granted our ability to make choices.

The power of choice will always exist. It is in this singular act of nature that lies both the freedom and the bondage of humanity. The power of choice is a divine ability that must be both developed and monitored.

The path of our everyday existence may not always be straightforward and clear. We are often confronted by many different choices. This can be overwhelming, creating confusion and uncertainty. While the forever-changing variables of life may seem unmanageable and demanding, they can be bested.

We are painting and creating our very own lives in every moment with our thoughts, actions and, yes, our choices. We are weaving the tapestry of our own personal stories. As we create lives of inspiration and pride, hiccups and bumps are inevitable. Challenges are an undeniable component of life.

Irony and unpredictability routinely rear their heads in life, be it in the familial, the personal, and/or the professional arenas. Life-long dreams often become real in the most unfathomable ways. Yet there are moments when our heart's desires manifest exactly as envisioned. This makes us nod our heads with fulfillment, creating indomitable self-assurance.

I am frequently asked, "Why and how did you become a life coach?" My journey was one of surprise, irony, pain and, yes, unpredictability. I would have never predicted that I would arrive at this very point of writing this book.

Becoming a life coach has ultimately fulfilled one of my deepest desires. The reason why is an inextricable part of the person I have become and the person I continue to become. Life coaching produced outstanding results for me—results that I had not found anywhere else. The principles and concepts I utilized were extremely effective. The implementation of these principles, with discipline, unequivocally transformed my life. This transformation validated the practicality of the theory. I studied the theory. I made the theory practical in application, and it worked.

The application of the principles I learned then spilled into my everyday life. I learned valuable lessons. I became equipped with the most useful knowledge and applied it. My courage and tenacity increased. This vindicated my previous skepticism. This experience opened new doors of understanding and awareness. I was now looking at my life with new meaning. My perception and beliefs about myself and the world began to shift.

And as my perceptions and beliefs began to change, my thinking began to change. The mind is the mediator between you and everything that you want to manifest in your life. This is the most important principle that I began to see and experience as truth. We are our thoughts. This will never change. And we have choice. We must choose our thoughts with mindful vigor and tenacity if we are to achieve the heights of our true potential. This is the greatest truth I have come to learn. This is the greatest truth I work to impart to all my clients.

The challenges of life are universal. The principles and practical lessons of life coaching transcend gender, race, sexuality, religion, etc. They speak universal truth. And they work. The only thing required is a decision, a choice to apply them with commitment. Life coaching can help anyone as long as they make the choice. Your choice. Your decision. Your commitment. This is all that is needed.

My life has been a steady stream of ripple effects, one after the other. When I say ripple effects I really mean cause and effect. More specifically, I am referring to the cause and effect of my CHOICES and DECISIONS and how they have rippled through my life.

It still amazes me just how significantly the simplest events can truly affect one. Perhaps, the truer statement is that one's reactions to life, manifested as choices and decisions, are far more influential than one realizes.

It is therefore not amiss to say that decision-making is a skill. Our CHOICES and DECISIONS shape us. One simple moment can lead to life long decisions with far reaching impact. We must all work to cultivate an awareness of the impact of the power of choice.

The cumulative effect of my CHOICES and DECISIONS led me to truly long for a better, truer version of myself. I yearned to create a new and improved version of myself. I had always sought out healing and a real route to self-discovery. Taking authentic action on the desire to improve myself and my life is how I ended up here.

Perhaps the above words will resonate more with you if you knew more about my journey.

Chapter 2 – My Story

I begin my story at a point in my late teenage years. I was 19 years old and I went through a very tough break-up. I was heart-broken, as many teens can be when this happens. While it is easy to dismiss my break-up and the resulting sadness as a typical teenage problem, it was a devastating loss for me.

I lacked the maturity and even awareness to effectively manage the depth of my disappointment. I had no tools to handle the devastation I felt or any of my other emotional responses. All of this, coupled with the vulnerability of my youth, left me feeling hopeless with no real help.

I found myself at a very dangerous precipice. With my lack of maturity and with little knowledge I fell on the side of confusion. I fell on the side of self-doubt. I was already discontented, seeing as I had never really liked school. I was also feeling tremendous pressure because I still hadn't discovered—or shall I say created—my place in the world.

The break-up created even greater unsteadiness. When my relationship ended, I was left in the lurch. I slipped deeper and deeper into a lonely depression and sadness. I had no idea where to turn for help or support.

I grew up in Corning, a very small town in northern California. Corning is a great place. Everyone there, including my own family, are good, hardworking loving people. My parents and my younger brother, Joseph, have always been incredibly supportive. I worked for my parents as an employee at their property management firm for many years (a great blessing and fortune). They were always by my side, even in my darkest moments. I say all this to point out that I was not without support at this time or at any time in my life.

The truth is, I never told them about the break-up or how devastated I felt. I guess I thought they wouldn't understand my feelings. I felt alone, so that's how I related to everyone. I felt alone in my battle so I just kept believing and behaving as if I was exactly that—ALONE. "They wouldn't understand," is what I kept telling myself. So I never let them in or asked them for help.

Perhaps my family would have willingly offered me emotional support. I just wasn't willing to see that. So, I simply never asked for help.

Throughout this entire time, my feelings of immense sadness and deep depression continued. I knew this was not normal. I began to seek help. I went on prescription medication. It didn't help. I still was not myself.

Though I was disappointed, I was determined to find something that worked for me. Over the next few years, I was on a conscious and continuous search to find healing.

Immediately after high school, I enrolled in Butte College, a local community college. I continued working for my parents' property management company. School was never my thing, so I left college and went to work for Media News Group's composing department. The composing department basically preps newspaper ads before the editorial content is added.

It became clear that if I wanted to move up at Media News Group, I needed a college degree. So I went back to college. I received two associates degrees from Butte College over this period—one in accounting and the other in business.

Working in the newspaper industry was very scary for me at this time. A tremendous amount of layoffs were occurring. I was determined to avert the doom of being fired. I worked very hard over the years to keep my job secure. I ultimately was promoted several times and ended up in a management position.

In hindsight, that was really a great gift, a great blessing. Even in my depression, I could function as a member of society without standing out as an outcast. Despite all the ups and downs I faced over the years, the tremendous work ethic my parents gave me remained ever-present. This work ethic was a gift.

I can liken my moments then to the motions of a rollercoaster. My emotions were constantly in flux. Stability was a foreign concept. I never stayed in one state of mind too long, especially the happy ones. I would feel fine one day and then very low the very next day. I was definitely going up and down.

Eventually, I enrolled in California Southern University to earn my bachelor's degree in Business Administration. I worked full time to help pay for college, as I made my way up the ladder at Media News Group. I purposely shied away from becoming emotionally involved with anyone over this time period. I was still battling my depression and sadness.

I tried all sorts of healing methods. I worked with counselors, chiropractors, hypnosis, hypnotherapy, acupuncture, etc. I tried anything and everything that might be a viable solution for depression. I was desperate for help. If it helped someone else then I tried it as well. My attitude was that I would find a solution no matter what!

My acute awareness of my challenges coupled with my proactive choices were extraordinarily powerful in shaping my life at this point. I knew there was a problem and I stopped at nothing for a solution. This was my saving grace.

Closing our eyes to the realities of our pain, sadness, and/or frustration, does not make it dissolve into nothingness. Choosing to ignore the problem, exacerbates it rather than solving it. Sometimes, out of a very selective and deliberate ignorance, we ignore situations. This then creates a hopelessness and false belief that a solution is impossible. There is always a solution. We must choose to see it. We must choose to find it. We must choose to create it.

It was just around this time, I began to learn about the concepts of affirmations and manifestation. These were foreign concepts to me. Out of both ignorance and curiosity, I decided to do my own research about these "new ideas."

Remember, I had already tried many avenues and none of them seemed to be working for me. So researching was a natural reflex for me at this point.

I told myself I would give "affirmations" a try because I know others had great success with them. I remember thinking, "This could be exactly what I've been looking for." I had tried so many other solutions. I was not going to give up now. Besides, I had nothing to lose.

I definitely tried affirmations. I said them aloud. I wrote my affirmations. I said them again. I wrote and recited them, again and again and again and again. Yes, and again!

I did not see an observable difference manifesting in my life. I desperately hoped this would be the thing to get my life on track again. But I did not see any results. Granted, it had only been two weeks. I brushed them aside. I concluded that affirmations did not work.

The unwanted sadness persisted for years. I never made a conscious decision to fluctuate so aggressively between happiness and sadness. But this is exactly what was happening. My emotional mood swings became a habit. They lasted for days or weeks on end. I couldn't get the sadness and depression off my shoulders no matter how hard I tried.

I would either be at work or at school. As soon as I was finished with the necessary task, doom and gloom engulfed me. I had no social life. I was very alone. The sadness and depression made me feel as if I needed to isolate myself. So again, no real friends or relationships.

I did not like feeling depressed. Neither did I fancy the feeling of being isolated. It felt very much like being in a black hole with no light. I often felt trapped with no escape.

The years rolled by and time, which is no respecter of persons or their individual challenges, kept right on drifting by. Fast forward. I was now 36 years old. I was still looking for help or a cure. I had spent the last sixteen years on a roller coaster state of sadness and depression.

I earned my Bachelor's Degree in Business Administration and worked my way up at Media News Group. After two promotions, I was now in a managerial position on a salary. I had accomplished these feats, but my depression and sadness had remained the entire time. It was as if those feelings blind-sided me to any of the positive things in my life. I never gave myself any credit for my accomplishments. I never perceived anything as positive or good, even it was indeed a truly good thing. Needless to say, my morale was very low.

I truly felt that I still had not tapped into my true potential. I knew so many more talents and abilities lay deposited in my soul. As far as I was concerned, all my energy for the last 16 years had been expended in a continual effort to keep the darkness at bay.

Around this time, I decided to work with a life coach. I had never worked with one before and was very hesitant. Nothing else had worked, so either the life coach would work or not. I still had nothing to lose. And I expected nothing.

This choice was the most defining decision at this point in my life. Even though I did not know it consciously, I had made a fantastic choice.

I started working with a renowned life coach and author. Together we began to unpack years of sadness and depression. With specific exercises and, yes, even affirmations, our work began to take tangible form in my life.

Six weeks into our work together, I casually mumbled to myself, "I have not felt depressed in weeks." And it was true, too! Everything had been going so well. I simply had no attention on my feelings.

It was very unusual for me to feel so stable and, well, to feel so happy. This was a stark difference between the burden I had carried over the last 16 years. The "usual" routine, the "normal," had been moments of intense sadness and isolation. I had grown to accept them bit-by-bit, even in my fight against them. Now I was creating a new normal, a new way of being and feeling.

For almost three weeks straight, I had been feeling great. This was a ground-breaking anomaly for me. Can you imagine feeling trapped for 16 years and then suddenly feeling the exact opposite? I felt a profound sense of freedom down to the core of my soul. The sense of release was exponential and absolutely unbelievably.

The dissipation of my negative feelings came from a very specific and targeted application of theories. There was nothing magical or mystical about the process. My dark and depressing thoughts dispersed with focus and hard work.

As a result of my coaching I was learning how to productively manage my negative thoughts. If anything, the magic lay in learning to take responsibility for my emotions and thoughts. I was learning how to turn my negative thoughts into positive thoughts. And I was actually doing it.

In the past, I would obsess over every negative thought. Unknowingly, therein was the crux of the problem I was trying so hard to solve. I was focused on the negative. I was simply giving my less-than-stellar thoughts the power to hold me for ransom.

My mind and heart had fixated on every negative thought and feeling. This kept them floating in the landscape of my mind. I would end up expending all my energy on the negative thoughts. I buried myself in the abyss of my negativity, which drove me into deeper depression. It was as if I could not find anything good in my life. There was nothing positive to focus on, as far as I was concerned, or so I thought. I allowed my mind to completely fixate on dark, discontented thoughts. Thus, I always found myself in a dark and discontented place. Do you see the natural and inevitable correlation?

Now it was a very different story. Or maybe it was the same story with me directing myself like never before. My negative thoughts did not suddenly disappear. They had become a fixation for me. I knew they would not just poof, disappear, or vanish overnight. They were still there, and crept up on me from time to time. But now I was in command. This was the gem from working with a life coach. These were the tools he had taught me.

I had learned a very valuable lesson I intend to employ continually. The lesson was to simply withdraw all focus and energy from dwelling on any negative thought. I was then to take all that attention, intention, and energy, and convert every negative thought into a positive thought.

This specific method made the biggest difference in my daily life. I was now focusing my mind on creating positive and contented thoughts. By extension, I became more positive and more contented.

Finally, the light led me out of the abyss of my pain. It did not matter that I had yet to fully grasp how to use it. I wasn't always perfect but I was doing it! What mattered was that I was applying my newfound knowledge and the numerous benefits I was reaping.

My personal belief is that no one event is ever really isolated or truly independent. Yes, this is the ripple effect that I mentioned earlier. We are bound to each other in a familial string that is invisible, but tight and sturdy. This connection transcends time and space. We may not be consciously aware of this, but it is there.

Imagine dropping a pebble into a body of water. The most visible and immediate reaction is the movement along the surface of the water. This motion eventually spreads across even more surface. The motion even leaves a subtle but noticeable effect below the surface. Actions and consequences. It is a relationship even observable in nature.

I could clearly see this ripple effect in life after I started working with a life coach. The results of our work together spread into every other area of my life. My very own life was my experiment. I am living proof life coaching works. I grew more optimistic about life. I truly loved the me that I was becoming. I now had something to look forward to each new day as opposed to the dreary emptiness of depression.

I found purpose and confidence and with this came a vigor to discover life anew. My age did not matter! What I had gone through could not hold me back! Hope bloomed in my heart again, and somehow I could bring myself to believe that I was a part of the master plan.

My life was a canvas. I had been hiding in the corner of my own masterpiece, as if it was like the proverbial ugly wallpaper. I was ready to let loose with my own colors and decorate my life. I found purpose. I discovered life again. I began to see that I could contribute to the lives of others in a profound way.

This is why I became a life coach. Everything that I have now learned is with the intent to help people overcome just as I have overcome. To this very day I still work with and apply the principles that I learned.

Nobody has a perfect life but some carry more burdens than others, burdens so heavy and so dark they have lost hope of ever being truly helped. Well, everyone can be helped. This I know.

After many years, I began living the kind of life I had always envisioned. As my life improved, I knew that I wanted to help others feel the relief and newfound joy that I discovered. This is the foundation of my work as a life coach. My life. My choices. My journey.

Chapter 3 – Thoughts

Thoughts are the abstract substance behind every tangible person, place, or thing in existence. They are the abstract components that make up every experience you have. While thoughts and your thinking ultimately take physical form, they are abstract. We cannot touch them. We cannot see them.

Humans are sentient beings amongst other things. Part of our experiential interaction with all existence hinges completely on our five physical senses. We see the stunning sunset. We smell the baking cookies in the oven. We hear the pleasant melody of our favorite song. We enjoy the hearty taste of a warm apple pie. We feel the soft touch of a wool sweater or a hand across our back. All these things we experience.

Thoughts are not experienced in such a tangible way. Let me be clear, however. Thoughts are experienced. Every thought is felt and absorbed energetically by the thinker. This energy is then emitted into the earth. This energy does not change until the thinker changes the thought. If this sounds ethereal and abstract, then the point has hit home.

Grabbing hold of the essence of thoughts can be challenging. Taking ownership of this can be even more challenging. We often lose touch with the fact that thoughts matter. We fail to see the influential power of our very own thoughts. We may even question just how powerful our thoughts can be.

Let's take a look at the power of speech, for further clarification. The notion that our words carry weight is not alien to us. We understand the power of words because we understand the consequences that arise from the very usage of words. We see the immediate result of our words. This is the case whether these are helpful or hurtful words. This is the case whether we receive or deliver such words. There are memories of the moments when mother or father or a school teacher stared us down because of the words we spoke.

The power of speech is why the President employs diplomacy versus going on national television and saying whatever he wants. He, just as the majority of us, speaks with care and caution. Preparation and structure often dictate conversation. I would dare say that we all use some caution with our words. There is an instinctual diplomacy that is often applied to the words we choose.

There is a tremendous amount of attention placed upon language. Words have direct and immediate consequences. We are able to discern the effects, because we are sharing the exchange with another person. Thus, culturally, we give our words much more attention than our thoughts.

Our society openly acknowledges the power of words. The right words can change lives. The right words can change the course of history and the entire face of the planet. Do you now see why people are so careful with them? There is an open respect for words and the way we employ them in our daily lives. Rightfully so. However, we often neglect the importance of monitoring our thoughts in the same way. We have forgotten the order of relevancy. What came first, the chicken or the egg? Well, I can tell you the thought always comes first.

The thoughts that play across the landscape of the mind, become the sculptor of words and deeds. Many fail to see this simple reality. One may exert great caution over the words spoken, but this does not change the fact that thought gives birth to words. What you think about, the *way* you think about what you think about, will be reflected in your words.

Thoughts are private entities. No one hears the specificity of a thought except the thinker. It is as if there is an invisible presence in the room that is never fully acknowledged. The "thought"—the invisible presence—is then ignored because of its "apparent vagueness." But we know it's there. We tend to forget that thoughts exist. We then conclude that thoughts have no power.

Our family and friends are usually the first to draw attention and or react to our word usage. However, they are not able to consciously recognize or discern our thought patterns. After all, it is not as if they have laser vision to see into our unspoken hearts. Thoughts are indeed the unspoken words of the heart.

How beautiful it will be as we become more aware of the inherent power of our thoughts. How much better for ourselves and the world in general. *You are what you think.* A statement of truth.

Every individual is an amalgamation of every experience they have ever had plus their environment, choices, and decisions. Many would agree that this is an essential truth. Yet, each and every one of these elements, is predicated upon *thought*. Thought is the drafting pen, the paint brush, and the mind is the painter. And life is the landscape that the painter paints.

We are essentially thought. This is not meant to be interpreted as an elusive, ethereal statement. This is the very basic uncoated truth. Your thought is all you. It is an internal accessory not as identifiable as a particular style of clothing that another could find pleasing or offensive by eye sight.

When it comes to the reality of what you think about, you are both judge and jury. Your thoughts being singularly yours means that you are even more responsible for them. They are the subjects in your kingdom. You must choose to reign over them.

This book is about solutions. The focus will be actions and steps to help you create whatever you want in life. Yes, there may have been missteps and mistakes. Yes, there may also be regrets. Yes, there may be an enormous amount of regret. No matter where you are in relation to your life, change is possible. The precedent here is change. The focus is change. The tools are for change. Ultimately, every precept and concept that will be presented will be rooted in creating and maintaining a lasting change in your mindset.

There is a systematic lack of awareness regarding the role that thinking and thoughts play in our lives. We have underestimated the role that our thoughts play out in our life. This confusion is deeply ingrained in our society and reflected in individual lives. We have gone on to think anything we want whenever we want. We are then puzzled and lack the tools to confront the life we create.

The inheritance of free will, equivalent to the "right of thought," does not mean or dictate the effective management of free will or of our thoughts. This inheritance is a present that may not be managed effectively, even though it is an inheritance.

We ruminate on our thoughts in private. We indulge in thoughts that we know we would never say aloud. No one else is privy to the innermost wishes, frustrations, and desires that lay deep in our minds. The awareness of this fact creates comfort, laziness, and often cause for reckless abandon. We have the sole right to our thought and thought processes, so we often are carefree.

This explains why a person at a party or restaurant would feel free to glance at passersby while allowing all sorts of lewd thoughts to float in and out of the crevices of their mind. After all, there is no valid arrest for not thinking productively. The assertion that only you are privy to your thoughts may be correct. Furthermore, other humans cannot dive into your mind and extract your thoughts. These above truths are observable facts.

There may be a human limitation in regards to thought. However, the same limitation does not apply to the universe. The concept I am referring to can be designated as God, the universe, the All-Knowing, a higher power, the creator, and/or an infinite number of other names that one may be prefer. For the purposes that lie herein the text I will commonly refer to the higher power as "the universe" or as a "higher power." This word choice by no means negates your personal meaning or preference. Please feel free to substitute which ever word feels the most accurate and authentic for you as you journey through the pages.

The universe is acutely attuned to every thought that one brings forth and focuses upon. This may sound peculiar to you or even surreal. We all answer to the universe or a higher power. This could be likened to the force, the pulse of energy that sustains humanity. The universe is directly connected to our thoughts. This relationship between our thoughts and the universe is continually affirmed right before our eyes. The universe, the higher power, tells us that not even our most private thoughts are private.

Again, the universe is privy to every thought and consideration that one brings forth and dwells upon. There is a connection from the mind to the very essence of the universe. The universe will always ensure that what is brought to life correlates with the thoughts that precede it.

It's just like Santa Claus granting Christmas wishes. You asked for it and then you got it. You may have observed at one point or another in life that things seemed to happen in an eerie fashion. Somebody buying you a particular skirt you had your eye on for weeks. Now, mind you this person knew nothing of your

can act on this decision and carry it to fruition. It is our responsibility to change our thoughts to more positive and beneficial ones. This is a foundational principle that can have a ripple effect on others. The simple and subtle 'small' changes will magnify and drive forth bigger changes. There is an irony that the big things we focus on need a push from the seemingly small things so they move forward. Clearly, I am eluding to the idea that something as seemingly small as a thought dictates the massive changes we want to create in life.

Negative thoughts are a waste of time and energy. They do not do anything beneficial for you. They are also harmful to our health and overall sense of well-being. Negative thinking only births more negative thoughts. This cycle continues to beget more negative thoughts until the fertility of the mind has been misused and converted to a wasteland. These negative thoughts end up becoming a habit that we begin to feel we simply cannot do without. Then the bad habits become normal. It gets to the point where our preoccupation with negative thoughts becomes a routine. We then do not see any wrong in this habit.

The path to negative thinking is a steep slope. It is a very dangerous path. Before it gets to the point where it is seen as 'okay' and routine, it is wise that a person checks it. If it already has gotten to that point, there is a solution. The desire to change and the willingness to work for the change is the top priority.

Life is made up of the good and the bad, the beautiful and the ugly. There are always two different sides. Hot and cold. Night and day. Light and dark. Joy and sadness. Up and down. Ad infinitum. Thoughts are subject to this same principle. Positive thoughts and negative thoughts are bound by the same rules. Positive thoughts inherently build more positive thoughts. Over time, they act as fertilizers on your mind and you reap bountiful harvests. Focusing on and maintaining positive thoughts, plants goodness into the mind and heart, and a harvest shall be reaped.

Your thoughts have power. Like any other kind of power, the power of thought can be used for either positive or negative ventures. The effect of having negative thoughts can be severe. Take ownership of your mind and responsibility for the way it works. Do not get comfortable with brushing some thoughts away and viewing them as "little" or not mattering. The supposed little things that do not matter can become a monster in a person's life.

An idea is harder to reject once it has had breeding time. When an idea crosses your mind and it is positive, hold on to it and build it up. When it is negative, let it go! Focusing your mental power on negative things shackles them to your mind. Before you know it, you are a combination of different kinds of negative thoughts. It might not have been what you intended, but by letting the 'little' things slide, this can happen. You deserve better than that from YOU. Do not ALLOW your mind to be a breeding ground for negativity. The longer you hold on to a negative thought, the longer it will be with you. The longer it is with you, the more chance you have of it spilling into all the amazing dreams and plans you have for your life and then polluting them. Ditch those negative thoughts today.

Most of us want things done yesterday. In the modern world, everybody looks hurried. People hardly take time out to just breathe and actually experience life. This outlook spills over into our decisions. We do and want everything in a hurry. We conveniently forget the very important factor of time, and the part it plays.

Acquiring bad habits did not take a day or just a few days. It took doing the same thing repeatedly, over and over again, until it became a habit. It took days; it took months. In fact, in some cases, it took doing the same thing year in and year out. It makes me wonder why we then expect to lose those bad habits faster than we can snap a finger. It does not work like that. Just as the bad habit acquisition took a sequence of repetition, it goes to reason that becoming free of such habit would also take a familiar route— a sequential practice with the new habit we would like to acquire. Carrying out a particular act in a sequence takes time, right? Right. So, it goes to reason that backtracking from that detrimental habit will also take time.

Generally, it is agreed upon that it takes an average of 21 to 30 days to transform a bad habit into a good one. I know it might seem like a long time and I understand. I can state with total certainty this amount of time is so worth the lasting changes that you will make in your life. I mean, think about it. Basically, you want to open a completely new chapter of your life. You intend to throw out the trash of yesteryears and usher in fresh air. You intend to begin life anew. Time shall not be a factor that discourages you or derails you from this path. Focus on the long-term goal, the big picture, and that will propel you to begin to make better choices. Take decisive hold of your thoughts and to begin creating a beautiful and fulfilling life to show it. There are many incentive steps to help you be patient while creating your change.

If you have been focused on negative thoughts, have faith during the journey back to positive thinking. No matter the time needed—21, 30, or 60 days—simply commit to your change. The only right or wrong answers are the ones you decide. After 10, 15, or even 20 days, do NOT give up. When you give up at that crucial time, you lose time. Giving up after having started can only create more disturbance in your life than before. It is like someone on the right track who deliberately jumps off the train.

Trust your instincts. Keep your eyes on the goal and never let go of it. When you feel tired and frustrated, when you are itching to give up, remind yourself why you started in the first place. Let this reason be enough for you to continue. Giving up means you basically go back to square one and in a way that is somehow worse than never having started. At least if you never started, it means that you will probably never know. Getting started and quitting is like having your sight on the rainbow and then deliberately letting go of it.

I know first-hand just how challenging this path can feel. I have felt adrift and inconsequential in the midst of my very own heart and mind for years. It is a feeling I liken to being amongst the living but not living. There was no joy living this way. I was horribly disconnected from myself and, of course, others. Life is for the living, meant to be savored and experienced. I missed out on life and all the wonderful things presented for a good number of years. I learned my lesson though and I moved on. I am happy about where I am today.

I thought in a negative way for such a long time that I had forgotten what positive thinking felt like. I had created an atmosphere of unrest and negativity around me that grew into a very bountiful harvest of depression and a continual downward spiral for many years.

The whole point of this book is to help you realize that you are in charge of your life and you can take control of it. The driver's seat of your thinking is your throne from where you direct your kingdom. What thoughts are you giving a hold over your life? What decisions are you making? What sort of energy are you connecting with that of the universe?

There are no external factors working towards your destruction. The only factor you need to hold responsible is you and your thoughts. Both the little things you do and the big things you do go hand in hand to shape your story. You are your own best friend or your own worst enemy. Ultimately, it depends on you, whether you know it or not. Your successes or failures will be traced back to decisive steps you took at critical moments and periods in your life. The only common denominator between both scenarios is you. You have the pen and you are writing your story.

I wrote this book to help increase others' awareness. I want to help people make every day a purposefully day. With a greater awareness, I believe that we will all make a conscious decision to surround ourselves with positive energy, from the inside out.

I wrote this book to help you emit positive energy out into the universe, too, and then to have it return to you. You can build the life you want and make the world that much more positive at the same time. Remember, a negative thought only binds to you if you allow it to. You have the power to convert your thoughts into whatever you want them to be. Seize that power and wield it wisely.

I really do not care if someone you know says this will not work. I will not be surprised either. People like that are always going to exist in our world. The onus now lies on YOU to filter through the noise and pick out the worthwhile piece of information.

I am a living example of the potency and effectiveness of these solutions presented in the pages of this book. I am certain that it can work for you, too. You only need to do the work to get the reward. What does doing the work entail? The answer to that is the crux of this book: being positive and engaging in positive, productive affirmations and action. Doing the work means you give yourself a genuine chance to change your life for the better. Give yourself the 30 days it is going to take to change your life. Thirty days is not too much to ask to change the course of your life. Resist the temptation of wanting a quick fix, and ignore shortcuts. It would be more beneficial to be done with it all at once instead of having to start all over again.

Continue on even when you feel like you are at your wit's end because, usually, that is the moment when the story changes in your favor. I sometimes imagine how much more bright our world would be if we had all stuck to our guns and crossed the finish line. The whole reason you are reading this book is to make a change. Make a choice not to be another statistic of one who fell off by the roadside. Do not let your effort be in vain.

Make the change for your loved ones who want to see you happy and living the life you want. But more importantly, make the change for yourself. It can be frustrating. It can be draining. But I can assure you that it will always be worth it. Make the decision today so that in another 5 years, you can thank yourself for making one of the best decisions of your life.

If you truly want to carry out a complete overhaul of your life, the first step would be honestly reviewing your thought pattern. What do you think about? How often do you think about it? Is there a particular trigger that makes you think in that particular way? Be painfully honest with yourself.

The first step to solving a problem is in acknowledging that there is a problem that needs to be solved. Honestly review your response to each of the questions above. Are your thoughts worthy thoughts? Are they positive? Do they add any sort of value to your life?

If you answer "no" to any of these, then you need to ditch that line of thought, as it is toxic for you. You need to consciously revamp your thinking process as a whole.

This book will help guide the way.

Chapter 4 – Part I –
An Introduction to Affirmations

One of the most commonly-used healing methodologies of this New Age are affirmations. Affirmations can be defined as "the action of imbibing the habit of positive thinking in oneself." The word "imbibing" connotes the action of absorbing and assimilating new ideas or concepts.

The ultimate goal is that the new idea or concept becomes embedded into of one's everyday consciousness. Thus, the new positive idea will then begin to influence and inform one's actions. The expectancy is that this will invariably lead to a new level of self-empowerment.

The practical application of affirmations is not limited to certain part of living. The embodiment and ownership of the habit of positive thinking can lead to success in any aspect of human endeavors. Essentially speaking, affirmations are positive and productive thoughts. They are a sort of fertilizer for the field of your mind.

If an affirmation is present, then this means you are in the present. Clearly, you are aware of your current circumstances. Clearly, you are also aware of the circumstances you want to create in the future. There is a genuine hope for the creation of possibilities. This hope is now accompanied with a healthy dose of action (the affirmation). This is a choice. Herein lies your true

39

power.

Simply put, an affirmation is something you say to yourself repeatedly. It is "to affirm" something—usually a new concept or a new idea to yourself. Affirm means to "state as a fact, assert strongly and publicly." An affirmation that is stated to yourself or written, is indeed being stated "publicly." Keep in mind affirmations can be both positive and negative.

The art of the affirmation validates the precise role that thoughts and emotions play in creating our lives. They are the foundation of the world that we create for ourselves. If we focus on positive thoughts, the universe rallies round us, ushering in our deepest dreams.

There are no rules regarding affirmations. Affirmations are personal. The only condition for maximum optimization is that it be something personal and stirs passion within you. Ideally, your affirmations should address something that speaks to your heart and soul.

Chapter 4 – Part II – Are you Affirming the Positive or Negative?

While you may not have total and absolute power over every thought that flits across the landscape of your mind, it is indeed possible for you to assume command over negative thoughts. The onus lies in determining whether you will dwell on the negative thoughts or whether you will take control of your thinking.

The power of thought cannot be under-estimated. It might be impossible to ensure that only positive thoughts cross your mind. We may falter from "perfect thinking." This is to be expected and tolerated with patience and understanding.

I always tell people they have power to take control over every negative thought and convert it to a positive one. It will take a conscious effort, but it is doable! Every negative thought can be transformed into a positive life-giving affirmation.

We all may hear or say this popular negative affirmation daily, "I hate my job." This is a perfect example of a negative affirmation. While you might actually hate your job, affirming it to yourself or others does no good. It is actually very harmful. This negative affirmation does not help you hate your job any less. Neither does it help create an alternative for you.

The negative affirmation, "I hate my job" promotes and

sustains an attitude of dissatisfaction. Just as long as you hold on to either a negative or positive affirmation, it propagates ripple effects in your life.

Now, doesn't this sound like a scenario whereby you keep coming up short? I liken it to a hamster on a hamster wheel. People become stuck in a cycle, going around and around with negative affirmations. It doesn't end here. You remain focused on what you don't want. This creates more and more of what you don't want and more and more dissatisfaction. You then forget that there was a time when you desperately wanted or needed a job. You forget that there are people out there who would give a limb to have your job. This may not fully alter your dissatisfaction, but focusing on others may cultivate gratitude. This may help you realize that you're most likely in a better place than you were yesterday, and that you can be in a better place tomorrow.

In the meantime, do what you have to do with wholesomeness of heart even while exploring other possibilities. In short, adopt a positive attitude. Work diligently to create positive affirmations to help you make the most of your current circumstances.

When you make it a point to affirm negatively with statements such as, "I hate my job," you rob yourself of the myriad of opportunities that could be present in the job you disdain. You are divorcing yourself from the potentiality of the present moment.

Remember, you are always experiencing your thoughts. Your thoughts shape every aspect of your existence. Negative affirmations will not bring forth any good results.

Opportunities are always present. How would you see that when you have all but closed your eyes to any possibilities? Remember, diamonds are found buried in the earth. They must sustain tremendous pressure deep in the earth.

My goal for you is that you begin to lean much more towards the "productive" end of the scale with your thinking. My desire is that you make a greater commitment to controlling your thinking and reap those rewards.

Be conscious and begin to make a concerted effort to take command of any negative thoughts. This is simply the process of converting them to positive affirmations. Tell yourself you can do it. Then go right ahead and do it.

Hold yourself accountable. Be aware of moments when you focus on negative thoughts. Make the cultivation of this awareness a way of life. When you falter, simply acknowledge that it happened. Take a moment to think back and reflect on how it happened. Ask yourself, did something trigger this negative thought? What was your mind focusing on when it happened?

This new information can be the foundation on which you rest. Anyone who can identify their triggers is in a great position. This new information is a piece in the puzzle. Use this information to help steer towards the lighthouse of controlling your own thoughts.

If at any time, you hit a rough spot, renew your commitment to mastering your mind. Let it be a method you eat, drink and breathe. Suffice it to say, let it be a way of life. Work with diligence to become at one with the art of positive affirmations.

We conveniently forget that most things of useful and lasting value take time to build. Once built their structure becomes so strong it cannot be torn down. A methodology that works for you today, but does not tomorrow, is not worth it. We usually do not stop to think about the feasibility and sustainability of those quick fixes. This is important to consider as you begin your journey.

It is important to mentally prepare for the reality that any form of lasting change will take some time. The utilization of positive affirmations is no exception. It is generally agreed that it takes 21 days to make a lasting change. This might seem too long. Remember that you did not start making negative affirmations in a day. Most likely this began gradually. It probably began with off-handed negative thoughts and statements and in response to a disappointment.

You began affirming negatively so often without thinking about it. You then adopted negative affirmations as a normal way of thinking. Now, you know it is a problem, and that is a victory of its own.

As you work to cultivate new habits, it is imperative that you be patient and gracious with yourself. If you allow yourself to grow frustrated or angry, this will be visible again in your thinking. You may unconsciously or consciously opt to take the ineffective road of venting your anger by affirming negatively. If you notice this, change it immediately.

The key again is to know yourself and monitor your reaction mechanism. This awareness will equip you to recognize and handle your triggers. When the low moments come upon you, it will be beneficial to recognize the cause. Cultivating this self-awareness is the deeper side of working with positive affirmations and is very powerful.

Whatever you do, whatever happens, do NOT give up. Stay the course. Giving up is never an option. If you persist, your future self will thank your present self profusely.

I wish people could see just how close they are to the finish line right before they give up. We all have a side of ourselves that begs us to give up. There is also another side. This is the fighter side that wants to win no matter what. The stronger side is the one you give the permission to exist most often. Make the brave choice. Persevere, grit your teeth, hold your head up high and stick with it. The reward is so worth it.

Make a conscious choice to change any negative affirmation to a positive and productive one. For example, "I have a great new job that I love," or "I love working with my new co-workers. We all get along really well," or "I am willing to see the good here even during the challenges." Can you see the difference? This promotes an environment for real change.

The implementation of positive affirmations does not necessarily mean your situation will change overnight. It does not mean that all of your worries will magically disappear. What it does mean is that you will have taken a step in a more constructive and productive direction. You will have given yourself the permission to start on a more fulfilling path. By employing positive affirmations, you are telling your consciousness that creating what you truly want is possible.

Many times, people stop practicing the act of positive affirmations because they see no immediate observable result. They forget one very important rule. Always remember this truth: Just because you do not see something does not mean it is not there. The changes might not be seen with your two eyes immediately, but know that the machineries of the mind and heart are working on manifesting them.

True change starts from within the essence of a person. The results begin to take shape inside your heart and soul. They then manifest outwardly. People are what they are in their most private of places: the heart and the mind. It will take some time and determination. The choice is always yours. Are you willing to hold on to a life-changing chance? Choices. They are such an inevitable part of our lives that have far-reaching effects and consequences. Think about it. Choose wisely.

Do not procrastinate. Do not give yourself reasons why you cannot. You will always find reasons, sometimes even without actively seeking them out. There may be a myriad of seemingly logical reasons as to why you simply cannot do it. You must bypass all these.

When I finally learned this lesson, I made a decision to re-visit affirmations. I made a decision to stick with it even when I felt like it was not making any difference. I worked every day on converting my negative thoughts to positive ones. I then focused on the positive thoughts every day. It was tedious. Even I wanted to give up. I refused to quit.

Let me reiterate. Affirmations take a commitment far beyond just a few days. You have to say them all the time. You need to constantly keep your affirmations in your conscious awareness. Keep your sight on them at all times. You cannot simply decide that you are not in the mood or that it is too tiresome. Remind yourself of your affirmations as often as possible.

Your affirmations need to be at the center of your consciousness so you can always act on them. Affirm your dreams continually so that the universe is constantly aware that you are chasing your dreams. Give your all so the universe can respond to your commitment.

If you only say your affirmations occasionally, it is like using a teaspoon to take water in the hopes of filling a large drum. More than likely, this level of commitment will bear no fruit. The art of affirmations is basically the art of re-programing your brain to think in a different way. While this is not an impossible task, it is one that requires a sincere investment of your time and will.

Here is a simple method for handling a negative thought that persists. If at any time you find yourself thinking negatively and you cannot seem to get it out of your head, simply say, "Cancel. I consciously cancel that thought." Repeat this until you feel certain you now can create a positive affirmation. Now focus. *Recognize* the negative thoughts. Grab hold of them and throw them out the door with everything you have got. Then consciously take hold of the positive thoughts and usher them in.

Yes, it is sort of like cleaning house. What better place to clean than your mind? Give yourself about five minutes to then repeat the positive affirmation. This can serve as an effective way to redirect your focus and flood your mind with positive and productive thoughts.

If the negative thought persists, just keep affirming the positive thought until it is gone. Take a deep breath. Release all frustration or annoyance so you are not tempted to simply pack up and give up. Your greatest friend is you. Your greatest enemy is you.

Positive and negative affirmations are like fire and water. They simply cannot exist together in the same place. Be secure in that reality and quench the fire of negative thoughts with the cool spring of positive affirmations. The ball is in your court. You decide if the positive or negative wins by the duration of time you spend on each. This is re-programing your brain to think and focus on positive thoughts. This is a vital step in revamping your thinking.

Chapter 4 – Part III – Working with Your Affirmations

In this next section, we are going to practice changing a few negative affirmations to positive ones. This is simply meant to serve as an example and a template for guidance. You must always design your affirmations to express the individuality of your heart's desire.

The common denominator of all negative affirmation is destructive creativity. Negative affirmations are a creative force. They create exactly what you don't want. Transforming them into positive ones is the first step to taking responsibility for yourself, your life and what you truly want.

"I will never find love" is a classic example of a negative affirmation. Here is the positive version of this affirmation: "Yes, I have an excellent new relationship. He or she will support me in every way." Now doesn't that feel much more productive?

Let's convert the negative affirmation, "I am depressed all the time." Whether or not you feel depressed *all* the time, once you make this negative affirmation a habit you will feel depressed *all* the time.

A positive affirmation could take this form, "Yes, I am happy and vibrant. Yes, I am full of love for myself. Yes, I am full of

49

love for all of life."

Converting a negative affirmation to a positive one simply takes honesty and bravery. It is all about being honest about what you want. It is all about being brave enough to reach for your heart's desire.

The universe will support you in every way. The universe will encourage you with signs and even human assistance as you take this journey. If you believe it sincerely, affirm it, and work towards it. The universe will step in and build the bridge between your thoughts, your positive affirmations, and the reality of your situation.

The world is in NEED of you and the vast deposits of greatness inside of you. Discover yourself, and affirm your dreams (even the ones you are scared to) into reality. The world needs YOU.

We are human beings. Facing and transcending the challenges of life is a part of living. It is in your thinking, taking command of your mind, that you see your power begin to take form. Be willing to own this power.

I can hear the thoughts taking shelter in your mind. "Is this really possible?" "But I can't feel happy all the time." Well, you are right, and I am not saying you are not going to have negative thoughts or be sad.

Say the affirmations all the time even when you do not feel like saying them. This way, your thinking will gradually change, and by extension, your thoughts. This will have a direct effect on your life

Again, this is not magic. Hence, it will not simply happen at the snap of the fingers. Do not be discouraged or intimidated by this fact. What of real, lasting value ever happens at the snap of a finger?

Be one with your affirmations. Breathe them. Exist in them. Be them. Allow your present and deeper consciousness to become one with your heart's desire. Say your affirmations verbally. Let your world be one with it.

Remind yourself of the possibilities that abound in the world. Let this inspire your belief in and commitment to your affirmations. Believe with earnest convictions that your affirmations WILL come to fruition and they will!

Below are some affirmations that may serve as a guide for you as you embark on this wonderful journey. Affirmations are personal to you and hence you can affirm something that is special to you. These are just suggestions to act as a guide. Feel free to modify them in any way to make them personal, or to write your own.

- YES, I love myself fully and completely. I love myself and every aspect of my life.

- YES, I have a wonderful relationship. He or she supports me in every way and I support him or her in every way.

- YES, I accept all good things in my life right now. I now expect great things in my life.

- YES, I know that the universe will support me in every way. I know that I am one of the most powerful creatures in this universe.

As you see with the above affirmations, they all start with the word YES. This is done intentionally. There is an energy that comes with YES. It is an energy of hope and courage. I suggest this to all my clients because the use of the word YES will infuse your affirmation with more energy and zest. This in turn gives you more energy and vigor as you attack life. There is a force and aura that accompanies YES. This will give the certainty that indeed the power to change exist. I am not in any way implying that not using YES diminishes your affirmation in any way or that you must use YES. It does not. I share this with you because YES works for others.

It is important that you follow up your affirmations with affirming actions—ones that support your affirmations. You must consciously do what aligns with and supports the manifestation of your affirmations. This works to strengthen your mind and those affirmations.

For example, if your affirmation is regarding weight loss, you have to start by getting rid of all items in your refrigerator that don't align with the manifestation. Positive affirmations are a major step in the right direction. The next step is taking affirming action that corroborates your verbal affirmation. Watch the universe meet you more than halfway!

An important factor is to also visualize your affirmations. It is important that you see what is being affirmed in your mind's eye. If you cannot see it and cannot believe that it will happen, then it will not happen. It really is that simple.

Paint the picture of your life with specific and targeted positive affirmations. This will ultimately add value to your existence. I imagine that you have beautiful dreams of what you want your life to be like. I know I do. Give yourself the permission to see those beautiful dreams come to fruition. Let affirmations be your pilot.

Chapter 4 – Part IV – Writing Your Own Affirmations

Writing Affirmations

In terms of both the quantity and sheer vastness of the space of our planet, no two individuals have the same story. Every story is different in spite of seeming similarities. Therefore, the specificity and uniqueness of your affirmations must be addressed during their creation. You must tailor your affirmations to you specifically. It is your story. These are your affirmations.

Write your affirmations just as you wish. It is only befitting that they come from and speak to your heart. It has to be such that even when you explain to another, they don't "feel it" quite the same way. Own your life. Own your goals. Express both through your affirmations. Affirmations must be distinctive and personal in order to be optimal.

Both the nature and execution of affirmations can vary greatly. "YES I am living in abundance;" or, "I am kind and patient with myself." Or, "My trust in a higher power increases daily." These are all valid examples. Affirmations should always be positive. Groom your mind to be a beautiful fertile land. With the seeds of positive affirmations, you will bring forth amazing fruits. Paint the picture of your life with thoughts that will ultimately add value to your existence. I imagine that you have beautiful dreams of what you want to create in your life. I know I do. Give yourself the permission to bring those beautiful dreams into fruition. Let affirmations be your guide.

Chapter 5 - Manifestation

The interconnectedness of life is visible everywhere. No matter how hard we try to extricate ourselves from human connection, it simply cannot be done. Humanity needs humanity in order to truly live productively and happily. We need each other to simply exist and live up to our own individual potential and, ultimately, our collective potential.

There is a connection amongst all of us whether we know it or not. It is as if each person is created from the same thread that continues to extend more and more into the creation of humanity. Though we may never consciously know one another, we are all spun from this same thread. Clearly, each of us has sprung forth from a shared life source. We are all dependent on this life source for sustenance and vitality.

This does not mean that we will all have the same thoughts, perceptions, beliefs and or world views. We are all essentially created from the same core essence of love. Our paths overlap with a blazing sense of dependency upon each other. There is always something that can be learned from another. While we can work independently, usually greater results are achieved when we combine forces.

This interconnectedness I speak of precisely mirrors the relationship between affirmations and manifestations. Affirmations and the art of manifestation go hand in hand. They exist with an ingrained synergy. It would be extremely difficult to try to separate one from the other. Independently both are useful, but put them together and you have a revelation.

The pre-requisite for manifesting anything is to affirm it. Whatever you seek to manifest, be it familial, professional, or intimately personal, it must be affirmed. You have to say your affirmations as a catalyst for their realization in your life.

Life is a progression through sequential stages. These sequential stages are necessary for a person to attain the status of "adult" and/or maturation. The cycle of maturation often mimics the cycle of manifestation. The beginning stage is the stage of affirming. You must be able to visualize your dream in order to affirm it. You have to own it. You have to be able to "see" it happening.

Manifestation is another stage in the sequence. After being able to see it happen, you can then SEE it happening. This is the manifestation of your dreams. Therefore, it is not amiss to say that affirmations lead to manifestations. Without affirmations, there will not be manifestation, and vice versa.

In a literal sense, manifestation is defined as "an event, action, or object that clearly shows or embodies something, especially a theory or an abstract idea." The word manifestation is a noun. This is very telling. A manifestation is a tangible item or thing. It is the specific goal of your affirmation in physical form. Hence, it is a noun (a person, place or thing).

Let us take a look at someone who desperately wants a new relationship. They have been badly scorched by disappointment in the past. They may react to this past pain in a rather typical manner. "I was so hurt in my last relationship, I am never dating again." This reaction may deeply contradict their real desire. This reaction is not rooted in the truth.

I can greatly empathize with such a person. Hurts are personal and can run very deep. Some people are dealing with long-term issues that somehow continue to elude them. You can never really understand a person's story until you have walked a mile in their shoes. Empathy goes a long way, but it will never take the place of living someone's life.

Every human being possesses a highly adaptable survival instinct. This instinct is well-honed and very attuned to detect even the slightest threat to survival. This instinct dictates the impulse to shy away from potential pain or harm. This is understandable. Humans are emotional beings; some more so than others. For most, the survival instinct is always on alert, ready to deflect any possible pain-causing occurrence. This instinct is not always rational and logical. We may deflect and retreat from unreal harm based solely on past disappointments. We may retreat from creating human connectedness and manifesting our true desires. As much as we are emotional beings with survival instincts, we are also social beings. We derive pleasure from being around people. And we prefer to be in the company of people that we care about and who care about us.

This person may indeed fear being hurt again. But deep down he/she genuinely craves a deep connection with someone. There is the craving for a special someone to share life with, for that one person you can call your own. Fear can be a very debilitating emotion. Fear can hold your life for ransom and keep you at a standstill. If you allow it, of course. Again, *choices*.

The ideal relationship that he/she would actually like to be in, has to be affirmed in order to manifest. For example: "Yes, I have a great partner who supports me every day. Yes, he/she loves me just how I am. Yes, we get along fantastically." In addition, "I love myself fully." It is important that we affirm our self-love. Perhaps it is the most important, because the only way to truly receive another's love is to love yourself sincerely.

Ideally, you will be armed with the knowledge of self before embarking on a journey of attaching yourself to another. You cannot exist and operate as a shadow of yourself and then miraculously expect someone to view you as anything other than a shadow. It is easier for another to love you when you already love yourself. It is easy for you to receive this love if you have a foundation of self-respect and self-worth, being secure in your love for yourself can do wonders for all your relationships. You will not question why the person loves you and what exactly your "selling point" is to them. You will be able to actually relax into the love because you have a good sense of self. You understand why someone else would value and cherish you.

If you struggle with self-worth, this is a perfect opportunity to begin doing affirmations. The universe will send you signs of your blossoming self-love as you begin to affirm it daily. The manifestation of self-love will come in all areas of your life and eventually in the area of a partner. But, I urge you to begin here as a step to manifesting your ideal relationship if self-esteem is a challenge for you.

What is life without love in all its wondrous forms? No matter how often the concept of love is examined, it will always be sort of a mystery to us humans. Maybe that could explain our insatiable hunger when it relates to matters concerning love. Love is the fountain from which all forms of life evolve. Without love, life would be chaos. It would be a jungle where there was no respect, no consideration, and no order. Love brings about empathy, among other things. When we truly love, we and the world become better and better.

We are not going to focus on past relationships. You know why? Because they are gone, over and done. It may be a wound that once bled profusely; but no longer. The wound healed. You survived. Hopefully, you have or will harness lessons to aid you in the future. Our past holds lessons that can be very essential to our progress. Anybody with their eyes on a goal will not completely detach themselves from the richness of their history (even if this history is not perfect). It is more important to focus on the present and the hopes for your future.

We are allowed to reflect with intention and purpose. But I discourage you and all of my clients from taking an all expense trip to the past. The goal is to sift through the bundle of yesterday, pick the points worth picking and leave the rest where it belongs— in yesterday. Expending the bandwidth of the mind on regretting the past is a waste of time and energy. When you do this, you confer on your past the power to dictate your future.

You deserve better for and from yourself. You deserve the right to be free from your past mistakes and to live with optimism and hope. You deserve the chance to wake up each day with vigor and take on life, ready to conquer it. You deserve the chance at a life where you give yourself the permission to put to use all the amazing deposits inside of you. All of this is possible, but you cannot do it clinging to the baggage from the past. You have to let go of it. All of it.

The disappointments and upsets from the past will always be a part of your life. History cannot be re-written. However, the future is yet to be written. The future can change. Your future is yours to create. It is a blank canvas that is waiting patiently to receive splashes of color from you. Paint the canvas of your future with courageous deeds, courageous choices, and courageous actions.

Most people exist, but do not live. People are walking through life without any destination in mind. They float in whatever direction the wind blows them. They lack clear direction and no focus. Sometimes, people punish themselves for a mistake or misdeed they made in their past, but they simply had no clear purpose to dictate their actions. They punish themselves by holding on so determinedly to the memories of the past. They punish themselves by refusing to live a connected life with others. Purpose and clarity can remedy this any time. No matter what your past entailed, the future is another ball game entirely. The disappointments of the past can be the victories of the future.

It is okay to be sad a few times, but it is NOT normal to be sad all or most of the time. You deserve more than a life that is constantly enshrouded in darkness. You deserve the very best from yourself. You are the harbinger either by virtue of your thoughts, actions or both. These thoughts, these actions are all affirming a specific type of thought. These are all tools for manifestation.

It is my fervent hope that as you begin to work with the tools of affirmation to manifest your goals, your perception of life will shift. The perspective that "life is a journey," can enliven you to live with enthusiasm and hope. Life is a journey where even with chinks in your armor and the blows you may take, you can take on every new day with a renewed sense of vigor and hope. The tenacity to attack life with eagerness can grow and grow as you commit to manifesting your dreams.

If you are joyous and feel good, this will be expressed outwardly. People can usually tell the state of your mind from your outward countenance. Your joy and happiness will be a magnet for positivity. An aura of positivity can help you manifest your affirmations. A spirit of depression attracts negative energy and distances you from manifesting positivity.

You now know what affirmations are and why they are important. It is necessary that we remember also that affirming is not a one-time thing. It is something you need to do consistently until it becomes a part of you. Even when you're sick and tired of saying it, do not give up. Remember that the darkest time is usually just before the dawn. Do not give up on yourself. Yes, you can! Believe that you can and just do it. If you are truly seeking to manifest and live and experience your affirmations, then double down on them.

Now, remember to put YES in front of all your affirmations, as it works to make your affirmations stronger. So, I could say, "YES, I have a great partner who supports me every day. He or she loves me just how I am and we get along well. I love myself fully."

A key component to manifestation is visualization. It is important that you visualize what is being affirmed in your mind's eye. This means to get a clear picture of it and to allow yourself to see it. This is also about experiencing the feeling of attainment prior to the attainment. As you visualize the ideal mate, job, or new-found increased self-love, allow yourself to feel it within your core. Experience the sensation of it existing, allowing it to live in your heart as if it is real. See it. Feel it. Believe it. Allow it to become real.

It is as if you are a long-distance runner mid a marathon. You must always keep your eyes on the prize. In a long-distance race, no matter how tired a runner may be, they continue the race. One step after another. Each day after the next. Take it as it comes and strengthen your affirmative stance daily. Put yourself in a prime position to manifest your affirmations.

It does not matter if you are trying to get a better job or start a new relationship or make more money. Every single one is a change one would like to make in their life, and the process remains the same for each. It is necessary that you affirm positively and consistently so that your affirmation can become manifested in the chosen area of your life

As you commit more and more, you will see a gradual manifestation of your desirable changes. If you commit to affirmations and taking actions that correlate with your desires, the universe will respond. You will begin to see an increase in potential mates or begin to make a bit more money. This is an indication that the universe is beginning to shift to align with your heart and mind. This is a clear response to the fact that you yourself are aligning your very own heart and mind. Take notice of these subtle changes. They are indeed stepping stones and an indication of even more to come.

Let the simple wins and validations from the universe sustain your energy and spirit. If at any time your morale decreases, simply reflect on the minor manifestations and wins you have experienced. Let these victories fuel you forward with dignity and grace.

During moments of uncertainty, the technique of visualization can be very helpful. Simply take a breath and allow yourself to dive into the daydream where all your affirmations are manifesting. After this, take a very tangible action that aligns with your affirmations. If you do both of these, you show the universe and yourself that you mean business.

Say your affirmations while driving to and from work. Make sure you have an action plan as well. Make the most productive use of your drive time, cooking time, personal time, to focus the mind on affirmations and visualization.

I think the best way to imbibe consistency is to set aside ten or fifteen minutes every day as your affirmation and manifestation time. This way, you can totally concentrate on the affirmations during that time period. Give yourself fifteen minutes to totally immerse yourself in your affirmations. Can you imagine the possibilities? Fifteen minutes every day where you go through the process of becoming one with who you are in your mind, with no walls and no barriers. Utilizing fifteen minutes daily in that manner is pregnant with a lot of useful opportunities. Try it!

The purpose of the designated time period, is to enforce discipline and ensure that you take conscious steps towards the process of re-programming your mind. Even when you are tired and all you want to do is give up, remind yourself to commit. You must just continue. Winners do not quit and I know you were made to be a winner. Do NOT quit. The possibilities of engaging in your affirmations judiciously are truly endless.

You must consider your time in short supply and jealously guard it. Guard it for expeditious and lavish use of all we have explored thus far, and you will see your soul blossom. You will begin to see the manifestation of all that lies within. The world needs this and so do you. Invest the time it requires and then watch out for your bountiful return.

Chapter 6 – Forgiveness

The word forgiveness immediately implies responding to life circumstances from a higher ground or an elevated state of being. In a literal sense, forgiveness is commonly defined as "the conscious act or process of releasing resentment or vengeance towards a person or persons who have harmed one."

Forgiveness is first and foremost a choice. Secondly it is a process. "To forgive or not forgive," stated here very much in the vein of the widely-known Hamlet line, "To be or not to be." To choose to forgive; to choose not to forgive. We decide.

Again, the idea that is tantamount here is the power of choice. The conscious decision to forgive can be extraordinarily daunting and challenging for one.

There are some issues, offenses, mistakes and wrong-doings that are easy to release. We shrug them off with a subtle laugh under our breath. On the other end of the spectrum are offenses that fester in our hearts. These unforgivable offenses begin to define who we are and how we see ourselves and others. These festering wounds impact every aspect of our lives. We relate to ourselves and others, and respond to circumstances based on buried feelings of resentment and anger. When resentment begins to horn in on the happiness that one deserves, forgiveness becomes the only true way out.

It can be difficult. The key is to truly understand that the act of forgiveness is one of the most beneficial actions one can take for the benefit of one's own soul and heart. Forgiveness is about you. There is an innate liberation of your true self when you forgive. When we extend our hands of forgiveness to another we are extending this hand to ourselves. Perhaps the idea of forgiveness would be easier to own if people realized that the act of forgiving sets them free.

While the emphasis has been on forgiving others' offenses, this applies equally to forgiving yourself. Often it is important to start with self-forgiveness, for one cannot give something they themselves do not possess.

Anyone who wants a happy and free life must learn to forgive. Holding grudges—consciously or unconsciously—against someone or a group of people, takes a lot of mental and spiritual energy. All this energy could be better employed towards productive and noteworthy activities of your heart's desire.

There is a well-known metaphor that "holding a grudge against someone is like loading a gun and then giving them the loaded gun." The irony is the fact that the anger and the resentment—even though seemingly directed at someone else—is really pointed directly at the person who is actually holding the grudge.

The individual who is bearing a grudge ends up losing all their power. The perpetrator is again in a position of controlling their happiness and peace. This time around, they are specifically giving that perpetrator their power, the loaded gun. By holding on to past hurts and refusing to forgive, you give your power away. You allow yourself to be held for ransom, even if you do not know it.

Forgiveness is a process. Every process takes time; that is what a process is. It is the utilization of time to come to a specific point. The willingness to forgive anyone who has hurt you, is a prerequisite for better living. The process of forgiveness will be individual and personal for each person. The act of forgiving is going to be easier for some and more challenging for others.

Are you sincerely striving to create a better life for yourself? Will you offer yourself every ounce of support possible? If your answer is "yes" to either of these questions, then begin by doling out the gift of forgiveness. Yes, give it out as a gift, first and foremost, a gift to yourself.

Make it a bonanza. Grant it to yourself and to anybody and everybody. The secret is to know that you are doing it for you, not just them. Make the conscious decision to shed all the extra baggage of pain. This is the beginning of the process of releasing yourself from the torrent of negative thoughts that accompany negative feelings, such as anger, resentment and hostility.

Remember, you are what you think. The cycle is often as such: Someone wrongs you. This wrong- doing causes you pain. You hold on to the offense and begin to bear a grudge against said person. Now all your thoughts are on the pain and sadness. You will then create a world that revolves around this hurt. This is the least supportive act that one can take towards themselves. Your entire world will then be focused on the hurt. This will ultimately lead to—you guessed it—more hurt.

If one withholds forgiveness, then bitterness, anger and every other negative emotion will grow inside of you. This negative energy can spread to parts of your body. It then endangers your physical, mental, emotional, and spiritual health. It can eat away at the soul until the soul is a husk of the former self. And then one will ask, "What happened?" Well, what happened was the clenched fist of hostility remained shut and held forgiveness at bay. You thought you were punishing the "offender," but the greatest punishment of all was from you to you. This does not have to be your story. And if any of this rings true, your story does not have to end here.

Believe me when I say forgiving makes you a better person. This is the case because forgiveness takes strength. The individual who takes on and commit to the process of forgiveness, always comes out on the other end a better version of themselves. The commitment that it takes to forgive is very much a character-building task. There is explicit discipline that must go into forgiveness.

I want to be very clear that forgiveness can be challenging. But, again you will become a much clearer person when you forgive. Essentially you get to free your heart and mind from negative affirmations. The journey is having the faith and willingness to convert the negative affirmations to positive ones. The commitment is to a new perspective and viewpoint of past offenses.

Here is an affirmation for forgiveness, "YES, I forgive _____ for everything that he/she has done to me. I know that forgiveness is for me. I forgive them fully." You can fill in the blank with the person's name and also exclude the words "him or her" if you like. You should do this for each person who has hurt you, or that you feel you need to forgive for any reason at all.

It seems like such a small thing but when you do it, it is like removing extra layers of clothing that you have been needlessly wearing. Imagine the feeling of lightness and of freedom, both literally and in a much deeper sense.

It is essential to forgive others that have caused you pain at one time or the other. But, again, you must also forgive yourself. On your journey through life, you have probably arrived and remained at pit stops that you absolutely did not have to and that you later regretted. You may have made some mistakes or "bad choices" and in retrospect you cannot believe you made them. Whatever it is, forgive yourself.

No matter what choices you have made in the past, you deserve a second chance. Give yourself the permission to embrace this opportunity. Permit yourself to live a happy and meaningful life filled with positive thoughts and affirmations.

Here is a sample affirmation for self-forgiveness, "Yes, I am forgiven and forgive myself for all my past mistakes. Yes, my future is wide open for creation." Say this affirmation repeatedly to yourself. Live it and breathe it until it is part and parcel of you, until you can feel yourself letting go of past mistakes and moving on with life.

Making a mistake is human, but refusing to move on from that mistake and thus making another mistake is just a waste of time. So, enough of the pity party and "woe is me" routine. Get up and begin your journey of forgiveness and redemption.

You know the expression, "One man's food is another man's poison." I will say right now, that just because you think you did something wrong, does not mean everyone else agrees. Even if they do, your "punishment" is not life imprisonment or being dead while alive. Ultimately, it is your life and you should judge yourself per your criteria.

I do not belong to the school of thought that says you should simply forget you ever made a mistake. I belong to the one that says that you look critically at your mistakes and learn from them. Who knows, there might be a few life lessons that could propel you to higher ground if productively used.

So, it really is okay to forgive yourself for everything—all your mistakes and every single time you feel you should have known better. Making a mistake or making bad decisions does not make you a bad person. You are so much more than any one or even multiple occurrences in your life. You are an amazing person who deserves amazing things from life. So, get up and get going.

Life can be challenging enough, without you imposing extra baggage on yourself and wallowing in unforgiving thoughts. While you may have made some mistakes, you have also done some good things. Let the universe balance the scale. Do not employ yourself as judge, jury, and accused in your own case.

If you are having issues with forgiveness, I suggest you write out your feelings on a piece of paper. Write out how you feel, what you feel and why you feel that way. Empty your mind of all the nagging, disturbing thoughts that plague you. Do this writing exercise as often as need be. There is no cut-off. Write and express yourself until you feel a relief and an ability to start forgiving, even if a tiny bit.

Remember to write out the affirmations too and say them out loud as you write them. It could be in a quiet place where it is just you. With all the noise in our world, quiet moments like this are priceless. Let it be a chance for you to connect with yourself. Repeat the affirmations to yourself out loud 20 to 30 times. You could also make little post-it notes about it as a reminder. This could be tacked to your bed stand or dresser, somewhere you can easily read.

Commit to being the person who cultivates forgiveness towards self and others. Prepare with waiting hands spread wide to receive the future. Look towards tomorrow with a spirit of expectancy. Work on forgiveness, knowing you are creating space in your heart and mind for healing.

Chapter 7 – Relationships

I like to think of planet Earth as one very large market sprawling over vast geography and topography. The vastness of our planet can be inexhaustible, even for the most adventurous of us. There will always be little patches of land yet to be discovered or explored. The expansiveness of our planet naturally purports an infinite number of inhabitants. From here on forth, we will focus on *homo- sapiens*.

Humans come from different tribes with varying cultures and traditions. Some worship one way. Others worship a different way. Some do not worship at all. Even with our numerous, often seemingly insurmountable, differences, "There are only two kinds of people in the world: good people and bad people." (Yes, I borrowed that from a movie.) The only thing that truly matters when connecting to another, is the intention.

It only makes sense that in our journey through life, we will come across people who fit into either category. Meeting, interacting with and befriending well-intended people can truly be an enriching and uplifting experience.

In the same way, befriending or getting close to someone with bad intentions could open the door to heartache and pain. While no one is perfect, clearly some people do not have the best intentions. These are the people from which we must actively shield our precious hearts and minds.

No one is perfect, not even the good souls with whom we

share this earth. Yes, there are times when even the good ones will hurt you. There are times when even you will hurt others. This is a fact that we must all work to accept with love, faith, and tolerance.

Relationships are intended to be beautiful. We are social creatures. We are people driven by our connections. Our need to connect and our need for each other is the simple thing that binds us together. Sharing and experiencing a special bond with another human being is truly what life is all about.

The defensive reaction is to shut down as soon as hurt comes along. Our emotions form an integral part of our identity. When people feel hurt, the tendency is to act from that emotion. They often think the solution is not to put themselves "out there again." They then shut down. Some spiral into depression and sadness and begin to dwell on negative affirmations.

You hear them saying, "I can never find somebody," or "I'm just not good enough." This is only true to them because it has become an affirmation, but it is an untruth. The only way to manifest the truth that you deserve a relationship is to affirm it. You have to believe it yourself, with every particle of your being. A negative affirmation about relationships does nothing to help. One will ultimately find themselves behaving in alignment with such negative affirmations.

For example, a person that constantly affirms "I can never find the right person" will very likely never find the right person. Why? We are what we think. Our minds are fertile grounds for thoughts to grow.

A person who believes that they will never find someone will not even seek what they want or will avoid it. This is because they already wrote themselves off as incapable of finding someone. They have zero motivation to try and so they end up losing out on relationships that could truly have been wonderful. Any efforts to connect will unconsciously be thwarted.

No matter what you might have gone through, you can rise above it. Change your mindset and change your life. Convert those negative affirmations into positive ones.

A great affirmation for a relationship is, "YES, I am open and willing to accept a great relationship." And, "YES, in my new relationship we support each other in every way." Relationships with family, friends and/or, a romantic partner takes work and commitment.

The above affirmation acknowledges this dynamic. It acknowledges the possible challenges that will be faced during the relationship. It also includes an affirmation of a commitment to overcoming them.

A positive affirmation like this, stated with consistency and commitment, will change your mindset and your outlook on life. It builds you up from the inside until the results start manifesting on the outside.

In this case, you are consistently affirming your commitment to support your partner while building your relationship. Your mind chews on this continual assertion and comes to believe it as truth, and develops it, and before you know it, it becomes a part of who you are. Even if challenges then arise, you are stronger in your mind and you are better equipped to overcome such challenges. This ultimately makes for richer and more fulfilling relationships.

Relationships are stressful, yes, and the reason is not far-fetched or a big surprise. Science rules that opposites attract, but in the real world, there is friction before that attraction. Relationships in whatever form involve other people and therein is the complexity of them.

Imagine two adults, grown and set completely in their own ways. They each have a particular way of behaving and have relaxed into their individual prepared routine. They are comfortable with who they are; it is safe and familiar.

Suddenly now, someone threatens to change the face of things. These two people come together and they decide to create a relationship with each other. One world meeting another world. What do you expect? That everything would be smooth sailing and rosy? Well, if indeed you were expecting that, let me tell you categorically that you would be very wrong.

Change is a constant element in life. It would be necessary that these two different individuals make modifications to ensure their relationship work. Where before it was "I," it is now "we." There have to be adjustments made to accommodate that change. Some relationships get off on the right foot and stick it out. Some, on the other hand, hit turbulence that cannot be managed and this signifies the end of such a relationship.

It is, therefore, not uncommon to have some people come out of relationships scarred and wounded. Some heal easily and remain open to sharing their hearts again. Many hold on to the fear of getting hurt again. It is human to shy away from hurt. But YOU are so much stronger than hiding your light under a bushel of fear. This is where an affirmation can come in to work wonders. "YES, I am open and willing to accept a great relationship, one where we support each other in every way." This is a wonderful affirmation that can help create the space in your heart and mind for a great relationship. This affirmation will also help cleanse your heart so that you become free to give and receive love.

Relationships must serve to be supportive for each person. They are supposed to make you a better person. A relationship with the right person would add to your positives and help you work on your negatives. If your relationship does not add pluses to your life and that of your partner, then maybe you are in the wrong relationship. If you are stuck dating someone who is not right for you, then maybe it is time for you to make a change. Fear may be the chain that holds you to the same position. Dare to hope. Speak positive affirmations into your life and believe them when you say them. You deserve the best, and this includes even your choice of a partner.

If you do indeed feel stuck in a relationship and know you want to leave, then simply begin to affirm this change. The key here, as always, is to write an affirmation that fits the specificity of your situation. Here is an example: "Yes, I am willing to release the old. I open my heart and mind to receive a new more purposeful and healthy partner." Begin to utilize this affirmation daily if you feel stuck.

You must continue to foster an openness and willingness to find a great relationship. You must continue to foster an attitude that you can and will find love even if you haven't. Having a great person in your life starts with you being mentally present enough to see that person when they are right there in front of you. A person who feeds off negative affirmations will be blind to seeing a great person.

It is important that you declutter your mind. Pull out the weeds that may lay in the fertile ground of your consciousness. Give the fruits of your highest truth a place and chance to grow.

Let's take a look at the following example: Imagine that you were going about your daily activities and suddenly have a hankering to eat a green apple. One of two things could happen. You will either decide that you are too tired or too busy to stop and purchase a green apple, or you will decide that you want the green apple enough that you actually get up and get it.

It is unlikely that a bright green apple will be delivered wrapped to you. In this example, choice is a very important factor. What do you really want? The same analogy can be applied to relationships. People who are closed off won't even spot a potentially new relationship because they are not open to it in the first place. It's a path they are unconsciously unwilling to explore. This energy connects with the universe and this is what they then experience. It might even be that they wanted it very much, but were too afraid to go for it. Either way, because they did not want it enough to go after it, they most likely will never have it. The golden moments of love get buried at the altar of fear and negative affirmations.

The first step is to believe and accept that you can have a relationship that is fantastic for you and your love. Many people end up settling in life. This is based often on comfort and fear. People sometimes settle for what is directly available because they have conditioned themselves to believe that what they really want cannot be attained. They have fed into negative affirmations that limit and stunt their growth. Ladies and gentlemen, it is okay to have class. It is okay to make choices. You, right there, remember never to settle.

Be willing to accept great things in your life, including a relationship. Be willing to take a chance on people, albeit with wisdom. The heart is built for sharing. Human beings, in fact most creatures, are built for care, love, and affection. It is not enough to simply want a relationship, even though it is a start. It has to go beyond that. You must affirm what you want so it can be manifested as reality. You have to do the work of sowing your choice seeds. Water them and then watch as your garden grows into a colorful, viable one. But you have to take the first step.

Here are a few more suggestions for affirmations to creating and maintaining a successful relationship.

1.   YES, I accept a great new relationship into my life.

2. YES, I have great relationships that are mutually supportive, respectful and loving in every way.

3. YES, my relationships are wonderful and loving. My partner (wife, husband, etc.) and I get along great. We communicate with respect and love about all concerns.

4. YES, I love myself fully. I am now ready to love someone else. I know I have enough love to give someone else. I know I am willing to also receive love.

When you have manifested a relationship, it is important that you keep affirming your relationship as a healthy and supportive one. Now that you are reaping a harvest, you must continue to nourish the crops. One has to nurture the plant to get desired results. As you progress in the relationships in your life, there might be occurrences that derail or deter. When this happens, negative affirmations should never be a comfortable place to fall back on. It becomes even more important to surround yourself with positive affirmations, which in turn bring about positive energy. Use your mind to create the life and relationships you want. Fight for what you have created.

Affirm your new relationship as a wonderful, loving opportunity for growth and affection. Set a high standard. It is impossible that two people in a relationship will not have disagreements. Differences in opinions will arise and some will be stronger than others. This is why it is important to affirm compassionate and patient communication. This creates an environment conducive for respect even when disagreements come up. Affirming this consistently helps it become a natural part of your disposition. Even when issues arise, the "you" that has been modified due to your positive affirmations will ensure that peace reigns.

I wish I could dedicate the entire book to this topic. Relationships, sharing our hearts, and caring are what life is made for. These all require a 'whole' person. No, not a perfect person, but a whole one who understands the importance of self-love. The love you have for yourself will be the love that you have to give and receive. As you love yourself more and more, you are more free to love others.

Drink from the fountain of love so you can bless another richly and receive richly. Sometimes when we struggle with self-love, we attempt to shower love on other people. We do not even ask for anything in return. Nothing. A relationship can never stand on such a faulty foundation. It is important to delve into relationships with the most productive mindset possible. Do not be selfish, but do not be a martyr either. Balance is key. Always strive to give, but do not give so much that you forget to receive. It takes two people to have a relationship.

Always bear in mind that there is no such thing as a perfect relationship. A relationship is made up of people and people are imperfect. There will be ups and downs, quarrels and misunderstandings. The key to ensuring sustainability is to constantly make affirmations that will keep you focused on your relationship. Then take actions that support your affirmations.

Staying focused takes commitment this is why one must never think to settle. If you settle you are reaching for what is merely comfortable, and there is no joy to be found in a comfort zone. There are billions of people on our planet. Frankly why would you choose to settle? Don't. If you settle one day you will be faced with exactly what you wanted but did have the courage to own. This is where affairs and infidelity start for some people.

Affirm the kind of person you want to be with and the kind of relationship you want to manifest. Connect with that energy within yourself and own it. Build your mind up with positive affirmations about the relationships. Connect to the universe with this powerful and positive mindset. Being in a relationship with someone you actually want, can be an extra source of strength especially in the face of life's storms. The knowledge that this person picked you and did not settle is a point of pride and empowerment. The reason for that choice will be part of the glue that keeps the both of you together.

Be willing and open to a relationship and you will find it.

Chapter 8 – Health

We have spent a significant amount of time addressing and examining the concepts of affirmations and manifestation. These concepts are of absolute great importance. They deal almost exclusively with the mind. The mind is the central operating system for all of life. There is nothing that supersedes its creative value. There are, however, other parts of our humanity that deserve to be addressed as well. In this chapter I will address the entity of the human body, the vehicle for the human soul here on earth.

The human body is such a vital part of who we are that it cannot be overlooked. I am talking about the body in the most fundamental way. The generality of our bodies, plus the individual parts, are imperative to our self- expression. The body is an active visible means of communication. It is through the body that our spirits remain rooted in the physical world. For example, the mouth is a very effective part for giving life to our thoughts. Now, where do our thoughts come from? The mind. This is a classic example of the dependency that exists between the parts of this machine.

The mind is the control console for the body. The body is a machine with the essential function of action. An inhibition in the body demonstrates an inhibition in the mind. It is an absolute that any physical dysfunctions indicate an ailing mind. There is no doubt that addressing this with affirmations will have a benefit.

However, we are currently addressing cultivating specific relationship with your body from the viewpoint of ownership. Indeed, there is spiritual element to taking responsibility for the body. It is important to know that the physical is no less important than the mental, emotional, or spiritual.

While affirmations can help with addressing any physical condition, the current focus is on the steps that would predate such ailments. The body is a tool for your spirit. The body is a tool for your heart and mind. In an era of never-ending New Age philosophies, the body is often neglected for the pursuit of spiritual enlightenment. I advocate free will and the choice of a path that rings true to you. I also advocate assuming ownership of your health in a proactive way as an expression of your spirituality.

This translates to care of the body. This translates to proper eating and sleeping. This translates to dressing and protecting your body. This translates to making your physical body an expression of your self- worth. This is what I advocate to help manage the physical aspect of your spiritual existence.

No matter where you are on the health spectrum, the aforementioned actions can be applied. As mentioned earlier, actions must accompany affirmations to assist with their manifestations.

If you are facing any type of health concern, please know that I empathize with you 100%. I was in pain for 16 years. While my pain was not a physical ailment, it haunted me, creating enormous mental distress. I do understand. I wanted to reach into my pain and make something good out of it. No matter where you are with your health, know that I stand with you. Pain is pain. Physical pain, mental pain and emotional pain—I speak to all of those in this chapter.

I wrote this book because I want you to know that you do not have to go through what I did. And if your experience is similar to mine, I want you to know that there is hope. No matter where you have been or what you have been through, you can find your way to a better life and a better tomorrow.

If you are contending with physical pain or emotional stress it may very well show in your physical presence. This discomfort may or may not radiate in your personal space. It is most likely that some will overtly ask questions about the state of your health, while others shy away from the glaring question.

Some may handle physical illness and emotional distress with negative affirmations such as, "I feel terrible. I'm really sick." Others may attempt to ignore such sensations and do nothing. And yet there are others who, despite physical pain and emotional distress, will affirm health and life within themselves. They become a beacon of light and hope for others. We see the radiance of the human spirit during these moments. A human being who defies pain of any sort does so on the wings of fortitude and courage. They become a symbol of hope and grace for others, even those who face dissimilar difficulties.

The mind can have an amazing effect on the body. If the mental emphasis is the pain, the pain may increase despite medical treatment. It is safe to say that one's attention will remain on the pain and that will continue to be the most real thing to the person. One can seek and focus as much as possible on solutions.

The challenge of health issues can truly be aided by deciding to affirm a state of optimal health. It will take extra tenacity and faith. Here is an affirmation to help with any physical ailments: "YES, my body feels perfect every day. I love my body fully."

As a man or woman thinks, so he or she is. Make a conscious effort to remove your focus from the negative that might be taking place in your body to the potential positive. Convert every negative affirmation to a positive one. Even though you might not have an idea of what exactly is going on in your body, believe firmly in your mind that healing is possible. You can take this further by writing affirmations that confirm healing is already in process. Believe that healing has occurred and constantly remind yourself of that fact.

The crux of every solution is always the self. It is YOU. There is no blame in this statement. The self is the powerhouse of life. If this self has not been fully embraced, we are confronted with a plethora of challenges. An absence of self-love can manifest itself in an infinite number of ways. This is the underlying cause to many societal and personal problems.

It hurts me to think that a lot of people do not love themselves. This usually leads one to seek love or a personal sense of self-worth outside of self. This could stem from a myriad of reasons—a traumatic experience as a child, abusive parents, abusive partners, etc. Or it could just simply be the fact that one never took the time to know their own heart and mind. They never took the time to peel off all the layers and take a good look at the person within.

It never hurts to say, "YES, I love myself fully. I love me." This affirmation can be especially helpful for one facing illness of any degree. Look in the mirror and tell yourself how beautiful you are. Creating and cultivating a sense of self-validation can do wonders for the soul, especially during trying times. It is all well and good for family, friends, and co-workers to love you and support you. But what about you? Do you love yourself? Their "pass" mark is important, but cannot be the only sustenance for your spirit. The mark of approval you cannot live without is the one you must give yourself. Self-love. Affirm it. Let the universe know you mean business. You are the only version of you. There is no greater honor than to shower yourself with love.

Life may manifest in both desirable and undesirable ways. It may pull you down and then pull you up. Whatever the current circumstances of your life, you are your greatest cheerleader. Remember this truth. Again, *you* are your greatest cheerleader. Even when situations are less than perfect, keep your chin up. Take solace in its temporal sojourn. Better times are ahead. Believe it. Affirm it. The last thing you need to do is put yourself down or think of yourself in a negative way. Fighting a physical illness is already a pretty tough battle. Fight your battles; do not fight *yourself.*

Negative words do not belong in your vocabulary anymore.

Often sickness in the body is created by harboring thoughts of loss, decay, and decline. Now is your chance to build a new thought-pattern. Now is your time to build yourself up. Brick by brick. You may falter, but you will simply rise again. If you are thinking along a negative line, detour and change it immediately to a positive one. Please refer to chapter two if you need a refresher on how to change negative thoughts to a positive one.

It is urgent that you envelop yourself in the right kind of energy. A perfect way to do that is with affirmations. Cancer patients are often shown comedy films to help ease and diminish their physical pain. Laughter is therapeutic and healing. Give yourself the things and the people that truly foster joy in your life. This will affirm a spirit of healing and health.

You get from life what you affirm in life, no matter what the circumstances. This is a fact. The concept here is a boomerang. You get what you put out there. If you exude positive vibes, then you will attract positive tidings. If you exude negative vibes, you will attract the corresponding tidings.

I suffered for 16 years from depression and constant lows. I also affirmed my depression and sadness every step of the way. I would constantly say, "I feel depressed. I feel down." I woke up with those words. I went to bed with them. These words became my mantra, my steady companion. It is no wonder then, that my life became that—a cycle of depressing lows. Oh, if only I had known that I was the one perpetuating every ounce of my sadness. I was energetically digging a hole for myself.

Nature does not expect perfection of us. None of us are perfect. What Mother Nature expects is fire. Better yet, what the universe needs from you is the fire from your heart and soul. This kind of fire will birth courage and give you the will to look beyond your circumstances. In your mind, think of yourself as perfect and visualize your body as being in perfect health. Among other things, affirm positive health for yourself.

Maybe you are thinking it sounds so much easier said than done. Maybe you are doubting your ability to apply this to your health. I know quite well that maybe you feel completely helpless and trapped by your illness. I understand those fears and doubts, and you are not alone. We all have fears and doubts.

Success is found in the management of our fears. I understand the difficultly in learning to think a different way. I also know that this challenge, coupled with a physical issue, can seem daunting. We must work even in times of supreme trial to not grow complacent. Sometimes it takes extreme challenges for us to commit to change. While it might be painful, embarking on change in the presence of physical ailments can be remarkable and miraculous.

The important points you should always hold on to, no matter what, are—don't give up, keep going and never, ever look back. Today is your day. Use it the best way you possibly can.

If you are currently unhappy with any part of your life and you are reading this, you are still alive. If you are alive, then that means that you can still work to change things. No matter that circumstances, I urge you to use every ounce of life in you to work toward a more fulfilling life. Life will always bring to the forefront the fact that one is living a second-choice life. We often become comfortable even in the pain and disappointments. Nothing amazing ever happens in our comfort zones. You have to look beyond the fears holding you back and then take steps out of your comfort zone.

It does not matter if something is wrong with your body. Whatever it is, it is okay, and you can work with it and on it. Keep in mind that the one affirmation that you should never lose sight of is, "YES, I love myself fully." I cannot over-emphasize this. The essence of your self is you.

Another is, "YES, my body is perfect in every way and I love myself fully." Yes, your body is perfect. Forget the world's definition of perfection. Don't ever focus your attention and energy on what is wrong with you. Life is not perfect, but your outlook about it can come close.

For example, when I would say, "I feel so depressed today," it did nothing for me except create even more depression in my life. So, no matter what is happening with your body, do not give it the power of words. Do not say it; stay away from negative affirmations and focus on healing and building yourself from the inside out.

There are two things that are imperative from my vantage point when confronting physical challenge that I would like to mention as this chapter concludes. The most important one is to work from a space and place of compassion for yourself. You may be beating yourself up for your current situation. If there is one thing that is undeniable, it is that every human being needs and deserves infinitely more compassion and empathy than they have probably ever received. When I say this, I hope that this speaks to your heart soul and mind. Compassion must be bestowed in abundance upon yourself when besting a physical illness.

If this is a challenge, then begin affirming compassion. Here is a sample affirmation for cultivating a more compassionate disposition and attitude towards yourself. "YES, I am compassionate and patient with myself. I now accept everything about myself with love and compassion." Feel free to re-write this one or to write your own. But please, if you have an inkling of self-judgment, begin to affirm compassion.

Lastly, there is no shame in asking for help. Always seek medical care from a licensed medical doctor when you are sick. A lot of people lose out because they are either too shy or too proud to get help. Get help if you need it! Do not be beholden to fear. Work with your medical doctor and any other healing methods you are drawn to. But always see a medical doctor if you have any ailments with your body.

Do your affirmations along with your doctor's orders. Affirmations will help restore balance in your heart and mind as you journey to create healing. In fact, let your affirmations be the inspiration to help you reclaim your ideal state of being and optimal health.

Just remember never give up. If you don't see a change it's because you have not done your affirmations long enough. Remember it took me months of saying my affirmations to make a lasting change. Don't give up and keep moving forward.

The ideas I've shared here are all from my heart to yours. I hope that you find this approach to life that I have discovered is as transforming for you as it was for me. I invite you to set an intention today. I encourage you to start with just one positive affirmation, and make it your own. See where it leads. Add another. Find out for yourself just How Positive Thoughts Will Change YOUR Life.

Tony Palermo

ABOUT THE AUTHOR

Tony Palermo is a life coach based in California. He works with clients in person, over the phone and on Skype. Tony believes in the law of attraction and affirmations. Tony knows affirmations can change your life if you think in a positive way. Tony writes articles for the Huffington Post and Thrive Global. Learn more about life coach Tony Palermo at his website, www.tonypalermolifecoach.com.

Made in the USA
Coppell, TX
31 May 2023

17540188R00057